Great
Start!

Purchased with
Smart Start Funds

AT THE ZOO

David M. Schwartz *is an award-winning author of children's books, on a wide variety of topics, loved by children around the world.* Dwight Kuhn's *scientific expertise and artful eye work together with the camera to capture the awesome wonder of the natural world.*

For a free color catalog describing Gareth Stevens Publishing's list of high-quality books and multimedia programs, call 1-800-542-2595 (USA) or 1-800-461-9120 (Canada). Gareth Stevens Publishing's Fax: (414) 225-0377. See our catalog, too, on the World Wide Web: gsinc.com

Library of Congress Cataloging-in-Publication Data

Schwartz, David M.
    At the zoo / by David M. Schwartz; photographs by Dwight Kuhn.
        p. cm. — (Look once, look again)
    Includes bibliographical references (p. 23) and index.
    Summary: Introduces, in simple text and photographs, the characteristics of some of the animals that can be found at the zoo. Includes a tiger, peacock, lion, elephant, camel, parrot, and zebra.
    ISBN 0-8368-2225-0 (lib. bdg.)
    1. Zoo animals—Juvenile literature. [1. Zoo animals.] I. Kuhn, Dwight, ill.
II. Title. III. Series: Schwartz, David M. Look once, look again.
    QL77.5.S374 1998
    590—dc21   98-15402

This North American edition first published in 1998 by
Gareth Stevens Publishing
1555 North RiverCenter Drive, Suite 201
Milwaukee, Wisconsin 53212 USA

First published in the United States in 1997 by Creative Teaching Press, Inc., P. O. Box 6017, Cypress, California, 90630-0017.

Text © 1997 by David M. Schwartz; photographs © 1997 by Dwight Kuhn. Additional end matter © 1998 by Gareth Stevens, Inc.

Printed in the United States of America

1 2 3 4 5 6 7 8 9 02 01 00 99 98

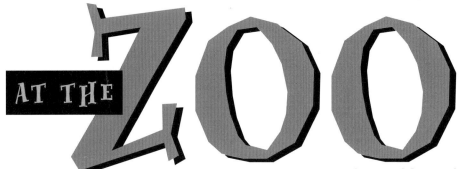

AT THE ZOO

by David M. Schwartz

photographs by Dwight Kuhn

A SPRINGBOARDS INTO

SCIENCE

SERIES

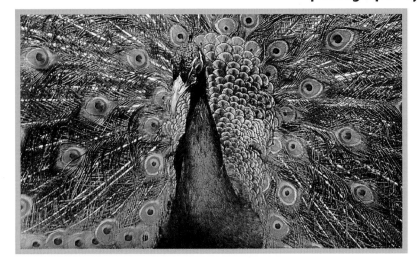

Gareth Stevens Publishing
MILWAUKEE

In the wild, these stripes spell danger! They belong to the world's largest cat.

A tiger's stripes are easy to see at the zoo. But in the wild, these stripes help a tiger blend into the tall grass, where it hunts for food. Small animals may not see the prowling tiger until it is too late.

This spot is called an "eyespot." It looks like an eye, but it cannot see. It's on the tail of a big, colorful bird that roams the zoo.

7

The peacock, a male, spreads his tail feathers into a giant fan. Only the males have showy feathers with eyespots. Peahens, the females, are dull brown.

The peacock rattles his tail feathers loudly so a peahen will notice him. He is one big show-off!

8

What kind of cat has
such long whiskers
on its snout?

The lion has long whiskers and a keen sense of smell. In the wild, the female does most of the hunting. A lion's whiskers help it feel its way through the brush.

These eyelashes belong to a huge animal with very small eyes.

LOOK AGAIN

The long eyelashes of the African elephant help protect its eyes from dust and sand. African elephants are enormous. Some stand 13 feet (4 meters) high and weigh 7 tons (6 metric tons).

Elephants have very little hair. They stay warm because they are so big. They do not need a fur coat!

Big hairy humps like these could only belong to a …

…camel. Camels with one hump are from Africa. Camels with two humps are from Asia. A camel stores fat for food in its humps. It can go many days without eating or drinking.

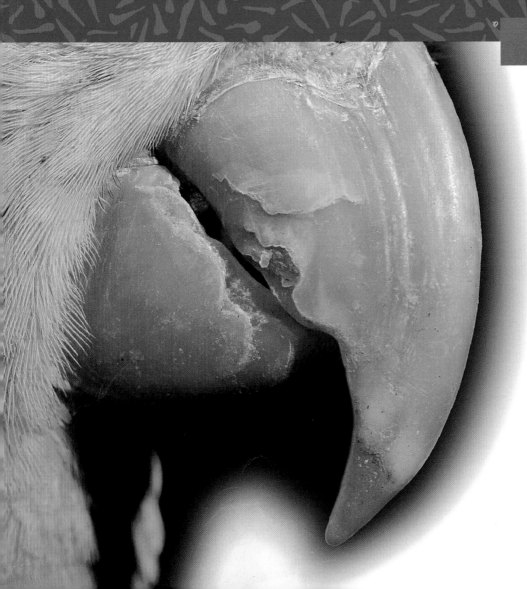

It is strong and sharp.
It can crack the
hardest nutshells.
Don't stick your finger
into this nutcracker!

15

LOOK AGAIN

The Amazon parrot uses its beak to open nuts and seeds. It holds food with its feet, then reaches down with its thick, hooked beak. Crack! The shell falls to the ground.

Where does the seed go? It goes down the parrot's throat!

Do you see black stripes on white or white stripes on black?
Only one animal wears stripes like these.

LOOK AGAIN

In the zoo, a zebra's stripes are easy to spot. But in the wild, the stripes blur when a zebra runs. Then it is harder for lions to see and catch a zebra.

If it is caught, a zebra will fight with its powerful hooves. Sometimes it can even kill a lion.

A.

B.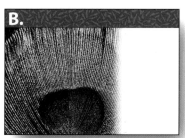

C.

D.

E.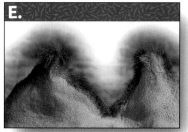

F.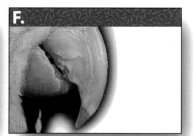

G.

Look closely. Can you name these animals?

19

LOOK AGAIN

A.

Tiger

B.

Peacock

C.

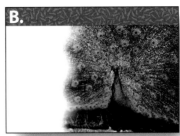

Lion

D.

Elephant

E.

Camel

F.

Parrot

G.

Zebra

How many were you able to identify correctly?

blend (v): to mix together or combine completely.

blur: to become dim or hard to see.

brush (n): land that is covered with thick bushes or small trees.

eyespot: the design on the feathers of some animals, such as peacocks, that looks like an eye.

hooked: having a curved feature that makes catching, holding, or pulling possible.

hooves: the tough protective covering of horn on the feet of certain animals, such as zebras and giraffes.

keen: sharp and strong; having very good senses, like eyesight or the sense of smell.

nutcracker: a device that is used to crack nuts open.

peacock: a male peafowl that proudly displays its colorful feathers.

peahen: the female mate of a peacock.

prowling: moving around secretly and quietly, especially as part of a hunt.

rattle (v): to shake.

roam: to wander from place to place.

snout: the long nose of an animal, such as a lion, that points outward.

whiskers: the long, stiff hairs that grow near the mouth of some animals.

ACTIVITIES

Zoo Mask-erade
Make a paper bag mask of your favorite zoo animal. First, cut out make-believe eyes from a paper bag. Add construction paper, pipe cleaners, and other materials to make feathers, fur, and whiskers. Use markers to add details.

Five-Alive Poem
Pick one of the zoo animals shown in this book. Then write a five-line poem about the animal, following these directions for each line:
1. The animal's name (such as *lion*).
2. Two words that describe the animal (such as *large, sleepy*).
3. Three action words that fit the animal (such as *yawning, pacing, eating*).
4. A thought about the animal (such as *Would you like some catnip?*).
5. The animal's name again (*lion*).

From Alligator to Zebra
Starting with the letter **A**, try to think of zoo animals whose names begin with the letters of the alphabet. You could also try to think of a word that starts with the same letter to describe the zoo animal, such as "big bear." For even more fun, make a zoo animal alphabet book with pictures you have drawn or cut out of old magazines.

What's for Dinner?
The parrot's beak is perfect for cracking open the shells of seeds and nuts. Other birds have beaks designed for eating different kinds of food. Find a book on birds in your school or public library, or locate some bird sites on the Internet that contain photographs. Can you tell "What's for dinner?" by looking at the beaks of different birds?

More Books to Read

Animal Survival (series). Michel Barré (Gareth Stevens)
At the Zoo. Douglas Forian (Greenwillow)
Elephants. Jim Rothaus (Creative Educational Press)
Secrets of the Animal World (series). (Gareth Stevens)
Zoo Animals. Eileen Spinelli (Forest House)
Zoo Clues: Making the Most of Your Visit to the Zoo. Sheldon L. Gerstenfeld (Puffin Books)

Videos

The Zoo. (Phoenix/BFA Films & Video)
Zoo Animals (series): Elephant, Tiger, Lion. (Barr Films)
Zoo Babies. (Agency for Instructional Technology)
Zoo Day. (Barr Films)

Web Sites

www.sandiegozoo.org/Zoo/zoo.html
www.primenet.com/~brendel/

Some web sites stay current longer than others. For further web sites, use your search engines to locate the following topics: *camels, elephants, lions, parrots, peacocks, zebras,* and *zoos.*

INDEX